WHOM THE LORD
LOVETH

The Journey of Discipleship

WHOM THE LORD
LOVETH

The Journey of Discipleship

NEAL A. MAXWELL

DESERET
BOOK

SALT LAKE CITY, UTAH

Library of Congress Cataloging-in-Publication Data

Maxwell, Neal A.
  Whom the Lord loveth : the journey of discipleship / Neal A. Maxwell.
    p.   cm.
  Includes bibliographical references.
  ISBN 1-59038-206-4 (alk. paper)
  1. Christian life—Mormon authors.   2. Church of Jesus Christ of Latter-day Saints—Doctrines.   I. Title.
  BX8656.M392 2003
  248.4'89332—dc21   2003014166

Printed in the United States of America   72076-7155
Publishers Printing, Salt Lake City, UT

10   9   8   7   6   5   4   3   2   1

To Colleen Fern Hinckley Maxwell
for her constant illumination, which has inspired me
for well over half a century now.
In our sunset years, she glows even more brightly.

For whom the Lord loveth he correcteth;
even as a father the son in whom he delighteth.

PROVERBS 3:12

CONTENTS

Contents

Contents

CONTENTS

ACKNOWLEDGMENTS

I alone am responsible for the contents of this volume, which is not an official publication of The Church of Jesus Christ of Latter-day Saints.

Several friends have been kind enough to assist in different ways and are especially deserving of thanks: Susan Jackson, for her patience in retrieving past words and processing new ones while dealing with my "unreformed Egyptian" handwriting; and William O. Nelson, Edward J. Brandt, and Max H. Molgard, for contributing a doctrinal review with helpful comments. Two other friends, H. E. "Bud" Scruggs and Elizabeth Haglund, reviewed an early draft of the manuscript and made candid suggestions. Suzanne

Brady of Deseret Book diligently performed the tedious but necessary editing.

As always, my only son, Cory H. Maxwell, was helpful in encouraging its completion. Having been allotted but one son, I am grateful it was Cory.

This book is better than it would have been without the touch of these friends.

INTRODUCTION

These brief lines focus on doctrines and scripturally based principles especially relevant to the course corrections needed by those of us committed to making the journey of discipleship. Because the Lord loves us enough to correct us, we in turn are instructed to "neither be weary of his correction" (Proverbs 3:11; 15:10). The format lends itself to topical mobility for the author and accessibility for the reader.

We all need more gospel *hope*. Greater hope inevitably flows from increased personal righteousness, all of which results from our course corrections and from diminishing our sins of omission. Surely Jesus' counsel to the righteous young man, "one thing thou lackest," was a call for one course correction in an otherwise good life (Mark 10:21; Luke 18:22). But will we have sufficient "faith unto repentance"? (Alma 34:15). Because repentance involves changing one's mind—which of necessity precedes changing one's behavior—pondering and applying the doctrines and principles are vital.

The Holy Ghost can teach us, completely and constantly, about "things as they really are, and of things as they really will be" (Jacob 4:13). He and the scriptures can alert and teach us, promptly and clearly, about any needed course corrections (2 Timothy 3:16). He can also sustain and encourage us as we pursue these refinements while strengthened by the nourishing fruits of the Spirit—joy, peace, and love—support so much needed in a world otherwise filled with despair, war, and hate (Galatians 5:22). We can access more fully than we do the gifts of the Holy Ghost, who "filleth with hope and perfect love" (Moroni 8:26).

Inconvenienced—even stung—as we may feel by the periodic reminders of conscience, these are part of the corrective chance given us to measure up afresh. Hope is increased by applying all the doctrines, of course, but especially the deep ones, which are simple and plain and declarative. God truly and personally loves each of us; He has planned for our happiness for a long, long time. Knowing this can cause us to be "brim" with hope. Evil will not rampage in the world forever unchecked. Meanwhile, we can check its personal effects on ourselves even now.

We can, of course, choose to spurn spiritual course corrections and divine directions, as did some ancients: "And the labor which they had to perform was to look; and because of the simpleness of the way, or the easiness of it, there were many who perished" (1 Nephi 17:41). Laman and Lemuel didn't really understand God's dealings with His children (1 Nephi 2:12; Mosiah 10:14). Such inadequate understanding of God's plans and ways causes some to look elsewhere, erroneously, to alternative ways, "which seemeth right unto a man, but the end thereof are the ways of death" (Proverbs 14:12).

The encouraging invitations to "plow in hope" (1 Corinthians 9:10) are surely there, including this

3

glorious incentive: "Behold, the way for man is narrow, but it lieth in a straight course before him, and the keeper of the gate is the Holy One of Israel; and he employeth no servant there" (2 Nephi 9:41).

The world desperately needs the leavening of righteous disciples, for many simply exist "having no hope, and without God in the world" (Ephesians 2:12; Alma 41:11). Disciples, however, see with the "eye of faith" (Alma 5:15), still perceiving divine design even when personal circumstances are shaken like a kaleidoscope. Jesus' counsel is to put our hands to the plow and "not look back" (Luke 9:62). Isaiah advises us that "God doth instruct [us] to discretion, and doth teach [us]" by "precept upon precept and line upon line," confirming the need for course corrections, so that disciples will "hold on [their] way," even in a troubled and turbulent world (Isaiah 28:26, 10; D&C 122:9).

With the help of the Holy Ghost, we can glorify Christ by repenting and thereby accessing the blessings of the astonishing Atonement, which He provided for us and at such a stunning cost! (John 16:14). Given what Jesus *died* **for**, are we willing to *live* **with** the challenges allotted to us? (Alma 29:4, 6). Are we willing to make needed course corrections? A trembling response is sometimes both understandable and permissible.

STRETCHING TO REACH
THE HIGHER BRANCHES

Happily, many of us have already picked and been greatly nourished by the low-hanging fruit from the gospel tree. Yet, on the higher branches, much fruit still remains, unreached for and unplucked. Neglecting to harvest this fruit deprives us of greater joy and of greater capacity to help others. This further feast includes, for example, those fruits of repentance ripened from correcting our sins of omission. The "cease and desist" portion of repentance is surely vital but so is doing the good heretofore undone.

The higher hanging fruits also embody the sweet savor of submissiveness, the nourishing nectar of consecration, and the milk of meekness. All these await our stretching grasp and represent the further expressions of love of God for us (1 Nephi 11:21–22). This fruit, said Lehi, is "most sweet" and will "make one happy" (1 Nephi 8:11, 10; 11:7).

No wonder God, who "delight[s] to honor" those who will so stretch, urges us onward (D&C 76:5). His own beckoning arm is stretched out and even extended all the day long (D&C 103; Jacob 6:5).

He knows all about stretching (2 Nephi 19:12, 17, 21).

CHOICE AND FULFILLMENT

Receiving ultimately what we have persistently desired proximately qualifies as personal fulfillment—widely varied though the individually chosen outcomes will be (Alma 29:4). By then, what we have become will have determined our capacity for joy. Our different-sized cups will be "brim" but differentially (Alma 26:11). We are the sizers and shapers of those vessels, and the potters cannot blame the potter's wheel.

There could be no lasting or real joy, anyway, if some were forced into eternal circumstances they had neither desired nor were now able to enjoy (D&C 88:32). Such an outcome would also be an unjust response to their choices. After all, Christ is the Lord of the Needle's Eye, and the words about the straight and narrow path—"and few there be that find it"—are His (Matthew 7:14; 3 Nephi 14:14).

Nonetheless, God's generosity will still be manifest. Even the telestial kingdom will be a kingdom of glory that "surpasses all understanding" (D&C 76:89). Furthermore, God's gift of the universal resurrection to billions and billions of His children will also bring an inseparable connection of body and spirit with all its attendant joys (Alma 11:43–44; D&C 93:33–34).

Granted, there are as yet unrevealed things about the interplay of joy and agency. Moreover, our present understanding is clearly limited about what constitutes a fulness of joy. Likewise, our appreciation of the fundamental necessity of agency in God's plan is similarly inadequate, especially since our agency and felicity are more irrevocably intertwined than we now realize (Psalm 37:4).

Sadly, there will have been many individual instances of "How often would I have gathered you . . . but ye would not"! (Luke 13:34; D&C 43:24).

In any case, our individual determinations precede God's final determinations.

God, a loving Father, is mercifully willing to give all that we are willing to receive. President J. Reuben Clark put it so well: "I believe that in his justice and mercy he will give us the maximum reward for our acts, give us all that he can give, and in the reverse, I believe that he will impose upon us the minimum penalty which it is possible for him to impose."[1]

NOTE

1. J. Reuben Clark Jr., Conference Report, October 1953, 84.

Having Character or
Being a Character

Some enjoy being a character, letting their eccentricity define their personalities. It is always easier to be a character than to have character! After all, getting attention is not as important as getting wisdom; the asserting of self is not as important as serving others. Yet, for some, getting attention is their way of validating their worth. Furthermore, focusing on being a character keeps us from directing our lives toward becoming the men and women of Christ by emulating His character (3 Nephi 27:27).

Those with sterling character, always in short supply, are invariably the high-yield and low-maintenance individuals who deflect attention from themselves to others—just as both of the two great commandments encourage and direct. It is too bad if seeking the spotlight diverts us from worshiping the Light of the World. Character, after all, is the composite of what we carry into eternity; it is not only portable but eternal. There is no limitation on such luggage.

THE LAST DAYS

World conditions, already grim, will become like the days of Noah, being filled with violence and corruption (Genesis 6:11; Matthew 24:37–39). Noah was "warned of God of things not seen as yet" (Hebrews 11:7). Prophets still warn "of things not seen as yet" but which are coming nevertheless. Seers can see the coming storms even when these are only "a little cloud . . . like a man's hand" (1 Kings 18:44). The world, however, being dim-eyed as to spiritual things, simply "cannot see afar off" (2 Peter 1:9; Moses 6:27).

The last days will be discouraging, with dizzying inversions of good being called evil, and evil good (Isaiah 5:20; 2 Nephi 2:5; 15:20; D&C 64:16). This form of vertigo produces worldly individuals who either have trouble drawing the line or holding the line against evil.

To help us, the Lord has "sent forth the fulness of his gospel . . . to prepare the weak for those things which are coming on the earth . . . [when] the Lord shall thrash the nations by the power of his Spirit" (D&C 133:57–59).

With the enemy "combined," it is vital to keep ourselves "in the right way" (D&C 38:12; Moroni 6:4). So doing will bring personal peace amid commotion, hence the reassuring counsel, "See that ye be not troubled" (Joseph Smith–Matthew 1:23).

Besides, the last days, however dark, will precede the glorious millennial dawn.

OUR DAYS

Nephi's record was "of my proceedings in my days" (1 Nephi 1:1). Thinking about our own days requires care in considering the past. A later Nephi wrote, "Oh, that I could have had my days in the days when my father Nephi first came out of the land of Jerusalem, that I could have joyed with him in the promised land; then were his people easy to be entreated, firm to keep the commandments of God, and slow to be led to do iniquity; and they were quick to hearken unto the words of the Lord" (Helaman 7:7). He sincerely yearned that his "days could have been in those days," yet he obediently became "consigned" (accepting) of his particular days (Helaman 7:8–9).

Whenever our time is, we can still make of our days "days never to be forgotten" (Joseph Smith–History, Oliver Cowdery's footnote).

Yielding to the realities of our days is actually part of spiritual submissiveness by recognizing a divine timetable in which "all things must come to pass in their time" (D&C 64:32). When we pray "Thy will be done," our submission includes yielding to God's timing. He lives in a unique circumstance wherein the past, present, and future blend in an "eternal now."[1] Those of us who need to wear mere wristwatches should be reluctant, therefore, to insist on our timetables for Him.

NOTE

1. Joseph Smith, *Teachings of the Prophet Joseph Smith,* sel. Joseph Fielding Smith (Salt Lake City: Deseret Book, 1976), 220.

COMMOTION

In a time when "all things shall be in commotion" (D&C 88:91), it will take the anchoring rivets of the Restoration to keep things from buckling, bending, and sliding. When things slide, they always slide down, never up!

To meet such turbulence, becoming "grounded," "rooted," "stablished," and "settled" is surely the remedy (Colossians 1:23; 2:6-7). Otherwise, the latter-day shakings will jar us loose; it is merely a matter of time. Pervasive commotion features geometric swings away from traditional moral values. Moreover, preoccupation with the fleeting cares of the world will keep us from navigating by the Light of the World.

Jesus' calming counsel is very specific to His followers: "Be not terrified," "I will be in your midst," "I will lead you along" (Luke 21:9; D&C 49:27; 78:18). God has promised to be with us in our "time of trouble" (D&C 3:8).

SALT AND SAVOR

The true disciple knows that he is to persist and endure not only for his own sake but also for the sake of others. Hence the admonition about the salt's not losing its savor, else "wherewith shall [the earth] be salted?" (Matthew 5:13).

"Savor" represents a spiritual seasoning and distinctiveness. Without it, the vital process of discipleship ceases. Commitment then becomes stale and flat. Travelers along the path become "wearied . . . in [their] minds" (Hebrews 12:3), where faith can go before legs.

BLESSINGS LARGE AND SMALL

When, like a big boulder, a large blessing rolls visibly into place, it is certainly noticed, appreciated, and counted. Meanwhile, however, the less-noticed, pebble-sized blessings mount up, layer upon layer. Cumulatively, the latter may out-mass many of our large blessings. Those seemingly smaller blessings are the frequent, subtle signals that He is mindful of us.

Because both large and small blessings reflect the beneficence of God, we'd better be aware of both, thankfully and constantly, and make honest and full inventories. God's hand is surely in the pebble-like details as well as in the large panorama, and His ways of measuring are so much better than our ways.

Though He sends "rain on the just and on the unjust"(Matthew 5:45)—both the deserving and the undeserving—blessings are dispensed according to our obedience to the laws upon which they are predicated (D&C 130:20–21). Nevertheless, when God blesses us, He does it with the Malachi measure, and the harvest baskets are "pressed down, and shaken together, and running over" (Luke 6:38; Malachi 3:10).

Besides, for us, blessing size is clearly not as important as the Blessing Source.

DECEPTION

One less-noticed abuse of power occurs when some allow themselves to be intimidated or blinded by the persuasive skills and domineering sophistry of others. We have seen it on a gross scale in the consequences of the blood-drenched dictators of World War II. Surely, "when the wicked beareth rule, the people mourn" (Proverbs 29:2). Being taken in also occurs subtly and in small ways, too, whereby we see how those whose thirst for dominion exceeds their regard for others, whom they use repetitively and unapologetically.

The deception of others always begins with *self*-deception. First the victim, *self* then becomes the willing accomplice. We see it all too often in the power plays of business frauds, politics, coverups, and even dating.

Regrettably, there are also the enablers, who do not wear a warning sign about their sad and facilitating role. Our lack of awareness is part of their deception. Evil enablers think they can walk on wet cement without leaving their footprints and with no accountability. More self-deception.

How necessary, therefore, is the Spirit to help us to discover deception, even in ourselves.

TALKING AND DOING

Sometimes we get so busy discussing the doctrines that *talking* about them almost becomes a substitute for *applying* them. One cannot improve, therefore, upon the instructive words of King Benjamin: "Now, if you *believe* all these things see that ye *do* them" (Mosiah 4:10; emphasis added).

Discipleship and soulcraft favor deeds but without diminishing the importance of words, preferring becoming to describing, and exemplifying over explaining. Otherwise, though doctrinally rich, we would ironically end up developmentally poor!

Nephi's "I will *go and do*" leads to action and brings results (1 Nephi 3:7; emphasis added). Its counterpart, "I will *stay here and moodily contemplate my navel*," stirs no souls, indicative of those who are willing to serve the Lord but only in an advisory capacity.

BECOMING SPIRITUALLY SETTLED

T aking up the cross first requires denying ourselves the lusts and appetites of the flesh. "And now for a man to take up his cross, is to deny himself of *all* ungodliness, and *every* worldly lust, and keep my commandments" (JST Matthew 16:26; emphasis added). "For it is better that ye should deny yourselves of these things, wherein ye will take up your cross" (3 Nephi 12:30). Yet "deny yourselves" is not a popular message in today's world of "me," "more," and "now." Self-indulgence is seen as permissible if an individual contributes positively in another way.

Nevertheless, *denying* ourselves the appetites of the flesh daily makes possible the daily *taking up of the cross.* Such denials create and reinforce the self-discipline needed to "settle this in your hearts, that ye will do the things which I shall teach, and command you" (JST Luke 14:28; JST Matthew 16:26; Matthew 16:24, n. 24d). "Every worldly lust" includes wrongly striving "to gain the whole world" even while losing one's soul.

Given the array of temptations "common to man," the best way of denying them is by giving them "no heed," by turning them away decisively at the doorstep of the mind (1 Corinthians 10:13; D&C 20:22). Otherwise, if we entertain temptations, very soon they begin entertaining us!

Becoming settled especially requires our being settled about Christ, His divinity and identity. It is one thing, for instance, to be advised to avoid adultery by one regarded merely as a sincere meridian moralist and quite another to be so told by the Lord of the Universe.

Some are not fully settled, however. They go through the motions of Church membership but without the developmental emotions of discipleship. Superficial affiliation is not conducive to course correction. While many who partake of the broken bread have broken hearts, a few regrettably partake of the broken bread while breaking their covenants of marriage. Some give of their time and their talents but still withhold some of themselves. Some put their hands to the plow while still looking back. Some style themselves as Christians and yet do not really talk much about Christ, let alone rejoice in Christ (2 Nephi 25:26).

In contrast, settled disciples are not unsettled by what is yet unrevealed. Moreover, the spiritually settled have long since learned to believe "because of the word" rather than being motivated solely by humbling and compelling circumstances (Alma 32:13, 14).

Whatever the wounds received in the process of our becoming settled in our discipleship, He who was most wounded knows how to heal us (3 Nephi 18:32).

THE GARMENT
OF PRAISE

Christ told us to give our cloaks to those in need, which includes giving "the garment of praise" (Isaiah 61:3; Psalm 30:11). Those trembling and shivering for want of a little praise and encouragement surely need the warming caress of commendation.

It certainly won't happen if we pass them by and notice them not (Mormon 8:39).

Being noticed confirms one's value in the eyes of others. Being deservedly commended does even more—by suggesting that one's existence is of genuine value to others.

GOD LOVES
EACH OF US

The most clear and personal way for us to learn (and to be reminded) that God really does know and love us is through the Holy Ghost. "The Spirit itself beareth witness with our spirit, that we are the children of God" (Romans 8:16). In various personal ways, He can reassure us by the still small voice (D&C 85:6).

These micro expressions can be astonishingly customized. "Did I not speak peace to your mind concerning the matter? What greater witness can you have than from God?" (D&C 6:23).

Our past, including premortality, obviously shaped our individual personalities significantly, engraving the signature of the Spirit by establishing a special, spiritual resonance. "Saith the Lord, I will put my law in their inward parts, and write it in their hearts; and will be their God, and they shall be my people" (Jeremiah 31:33). "The work of the law [is] written in their hearts, their conscience also bearing witness" (Romans 2:15).

The Savior's sheep follow Him, for they know His voice (John 10:4, 16; D&C 84:52).

In addition to the revelatory reassurances of the Holy Ghost and our inborn spiritual resonance, there are very significant and comforting declarations to assure us.

"For God so loved the world, that he gave his only begotten Son, that whosoever believeth in him should not perish, but have everlasting life" (John 3:16).

Because of that profound gift of divine love, all mankind will be resurrected (1 Corinthians 15:22). In truth, God "loveth the world" (2 Nephi 26:24). He crafted this planet to be inhabited by us, His spirit children (Isaiah 45:18). We are, in fact, at the center of God's "work and glory," the very focus of which is "to bring to pass the immortality and eternal life of man" (Moses 1:39).

What could be more indicative? More declarative? More redemptive?

Christ, from whose love nothing can separate us (Romans 8:35), testified to His earlier long-suffering as Jehovah, saying in lamentation, "O Jerusalem, Jerusalem, thou that killest the prophets, and stonest them which are sent unto thee, how often would I have gathered thy children together, even as a hen gathereth her chickens under her wings, and *ye would not!*" (Matthew 23:37; emphasis added).

Even though unreciprocated, God's love has not gone unextended. His redeeming "arm is stretched out," and His "hand is stretched out still"! (D&C 136:22; 2 Nephi 20:4). Yet human history is filled with "and ye would nots."

Peter, in his sunset days, after all his enriching and soul-stretching experiences, counseled us, "[Cast] all your care upon [God], for he careth for you" (1 Peter 5:7).

Enoch, while glimpsing the glories of God's creations, received the one reassurance about God that he most sought: "Yet thou art there" (Moses 7:30).

Nephi, though puzzled over the full meaning of

God's condescension, nevertheless knew that God loves His children (1 Nephi 11:17).

Thus, through the Holy Ghost, God speaks to our minds and to our hearts (D&C 8:2). Likewise, through His many communications to us about His plan of redemption in His holy scriptures and His customized blessings to us, God conveys His love of us time and time and time again. He hears our personal prayers. In countless, individualized ways, God's loving kindness and long-suffering are clearly manifest to us.

Even so, amid His profound love for us, He will not force us to come home to Him.

Suppose

Suppose that you have been you for a very long, long time (D&C 93:29; Abraham 3:18). Furthermore, suppose that, in ways not now fully revealed, a loving God became the Father of our spirit, demonstrating that "he first loved us" (1 John 4:19).

Suppose, given whatever He did way back then, also unrevealed as yet, that God is doing the best even He can do, given that with which He began and especially in view of His having empowered us to act for ourselves.

Suppose, too, that God's agency-based plan is designed for our eternal happiness and that He will do all He can to help us choose, unforced, the path of happiness by meting out through revelation the spiritual secrets of the universe (D&C 93:19–20).

Suppose, based upon previous and foreseen present performances, certain individuals were "called and prepared" before the foundation of the world to be leaders designated to help all of Father's children (Alma 13:3; D&C 138).

Are not these suppositions actually revelations? (Alma 12:9, 30).

EXTRA CHALLENGES

Life's recurring challenges include the minor vexations, too. One is developing genuine compassion for those who are awash with self-pity. Better for these to receive our rescuing empathy than to be left to swim in their own self-pity.

Another is displaying greater patience with the chronically impatient, especially when our own impatience is clearly not conquered in a day.

Learning to love those we don't like is an even more demanding peak to be climbed.

Those difficult to love—and we may ourselves be such at times—can make giving up seem attractive, or at least bring a slackening and a relapse in our relationships. No wonder resilience matters so much. Trying again may bring the long-sought breakthrough, which is what long-suffering is all about.

There is no footnote to the second commandment indicating exemptions are available in meeting such vexations.

THE GREAT DEPRIVATION

If we do not know the doctrines, do not honestly count our blessings, and do not serve and think about the Lord, then we become estranged from Him (Mosiah 5:11–13). It is our decision—entirely.

There is yet another pervasive cause of such distancing: "Despair cometh because of iniquity" (Moroni 10:22). If living amiss, we will not experience the "power of the Holy Spirit, which God bestows on those who love him, and purify themselves before him" (D&C 76:116). Therefore, if His love is unfelt by us, it is because we have taken our phone off the hook, having in one way or another let ourselves become "past feeling" (Ephesians 4:19; 1 Nephi 17:45; Moroni 9:20).

If *unfelt* by us, it is not because God's love is *unoffered*. The remedy is within our reach, if we choose to reach out for and grasp His extended arm (Helaman 11:10, 15–16).

Abraham, for instance, left a partially dysfunctional family in search of greater happiness (Abraham 1:1–2). The prodigal son "came to himself," saying he would "arise and go" to his father (Luke 15:17–18). Others who have been doing honorable but nonetheless lesser chores can at last begin to put first the work of God by letting go of their particularized nets "straightway," soon becoming "anxiously engaged" (Matthew 4:20; D&C 58:27). Some, like Amulek, were "called many times" yet "would not hear" (Alma 10:6). But Amulek's introspection, when it occurred, was conducted honestly.

It is usually a particular preoccupation, not a specific occupation, that we need to leave straightway and without looking back.

Broken Bows

Laman and Lemuel were angry when Nephi broke his bow (1 Nephi 16:18). Yet Laman and Lemuel were apparently not self-critical when their own bows had earlier "lost their springs," nor is there any record of their trying to make new bows to feed their families (1 Nephi 16:21). One can almost hear them saying, "Let Nephi do it. This trip was his idea."

Life's broken bows can create resentment, as if we have given God a quota of irritants that He must not exceed. Hence, in our frustrations, some of us murmur over our own equivalents of broken bows.

These hyperventilating moments use up some of the oxygen provided by God's lending us breath from moment to moment (Mosiah 2:21). Because God has said He will try our patience and our faith, how should we view such irritating trials? (Mosiah 23:21). Furthermore, if there were never any broken bows, how else would we be brought to perform certain spiritual calisthenics?

Broken bows litter the landscapes of our lives, representing yesterday's frustrations. These were real enough at the moment. Dotting the same landscape, however, are many more reminders of blessings than of discarded broken bows. May we have the eyes to see that which an outside auditor would surely see as he counts our blessings.

MEMORIES

Warehousing and accessing good memories is a talent. We are given the promise that the Holy Ghost will "bring all things to your remembrance," most notably Christ's words (John 14:26). Memories properly inventoried can serve as their own "cloud of witnesses" (Hebrews 12:1), there to steady us.

Memories can be renewing and prevailing amid present difficulties.

> *There once was a dachshund*
> *Oh so long,*
> *He hadn't any notion*
> *How long it took to notify*
> *His tail of his emotion.*

So while his big eyes were
Filled with woe and sadness,
His little tail went wagging on
Because of previous gladness.
                    (Anonymous)

When nostalgia stirs us productively, glimpses of the past can refresh us. Never mind that amid the surf of recall we usually find it difficult to share glimpses of our own past with others. Friends see how certain memories please us and are glad but only vicariously. Our memories remain peculiarly our own.

Unless wisely accessed, however, memories can also be unduly enhanced; we can "warehouse" a mere "whisper . . . as a shout."[1] The careful cultivation of memories, for example, may not have occurred later for some who were little children when King Benjamin gave his supernal sermon (Mosiah 3–4; 26:1–2). Was the disbelief in the rising generation merely a reflection of their lack of understanding because of their childhood and the passage of time? Did spiritual memories go untransmitted because they were not "enlarged" by being incorporated in the collective memory of the people? (Alma 37:8). Or were the hearts of the young disbelievers hardened for other reasons? (Mosiah 26:1–2).

We need both the guidance and the timing of the Holy Ghost to help us manage our memories. President Joseph F. Smith said: "May I say to you that in reality a man cannot forget anything? He may have a lapse of memory; he may not be able to recall at the moment a thing that he knows or words that he has spoken; he may not have the power at his will to call up these events and words; but let God Almighty touch the mainspring of the memory and awaken recollection, and you will find then that you have not even forgotten a single idle word that you have spoken!"[2]

NOTES

1. Wayne Martindale and Jerry Root, ed., *The Quotable Lewis* (Wheaton, Ill.: Tyndale House Publishers, 1990), 424.
2. Joseph F. Smith, "A Sermon on Purity," *Improvement Era,* May 1903, 503–4.

FIERY DARTS

The scriptures warn of incoming "fiery darts"; unless deflected or extinguished by the "shield of faith" (D&C 27:17; Ephesians 6:16), some get through to sting and burn. Included are intellectual barbs dipped in doubt and deliberately designed to get under the skin.

Fiery darts may not disable, but they certainly can discourage and distract. Very individualized, these fiery darts can be like "time-on-target" artillery, thereby achieving maximum effect.

Yet we have the promise that "[God] would have extended his arm and supported you against all the fiery darts of the adversary; and he would have been with you in every time of trouble" (D&C 3:8).

No wonder the shield of faith serves us so well. But it had better be sturdy and in place!

Shrinking Our Choices

Yes, we are "free to choose," but, ironically, misusing our agency, such as by celebrating our appetites, actually contracts our range of choices. Addiction of whatever form shrinks our focus (2 Nephi 2:27). Misusing our God-given freedom to choose brings consequences that are not agency friendly. Some "push the edges of the envelope," seeking emancipation only to experience contraction.

Consider, for example, the case of the Gadarene swine. By the time that herd made their headlong dash to the sea, they would not have been much interested in considering options.

Increasingly, therefore, hedonists who herald

their liberty to choose do so while scarcely noticing the diminishing horizon. Hence, what a war was fought over in heaven, is, by some, surrendered so easily on earth (Revelation 12:7; D&C 28:36).

SELF-CONSTRAINT AND AGENCY

S ome of the world's most highly talented individuals believe, self-servingly, that mortals "[fare] in this life," prosper, and conquer according to their "genius" and strength (Alma 30:17). A few freewheelers even believe that whatsoever people do is "no crime," hurrying on to pleasure because they believe "when a man was dead, that was the end thereof" (Alma 30:17–18). Such selfish views are clearly not a climate in which the second commandment flourishes.

Self-centered beliefs hasten those circumstances in which "every man walketh in his own way, and after the image of his own God" (D&C 1:16). It has been thus so many times: "In those days there was no king in Israel, but every man did that which was right in his own eyes" (Judges 17:6).

Without a moral compass, agency goes awry. Strangely, provincial pride is then mistaken for genuine individuality. The broad way leading to the wide gate is well traveled, including by some self-styled rugged individualists who scarcely notice they are actually part of a crowd (Matthew 7:13).

Lowly High Achievers

God is a generous God, fully recognizing what His children do to help mankind. Even so, as to our achievements, there remains this humbling reality:

"Little people like you and me, if our prayers are sometimes granted, beyond all hope and probability, had better not draw hasty conclusions to our own advantage. If we were stronger, we might be less tenderly treated. If we were braver, we might be sent, with far less help, to defend far more desperate posts in the great battle."[1]

There was no more "desperate post" than Gethsemane or Calvary!

Because our imperfections thus limit our

contributions, the more we become like Him, the more we can do to help. How many more gifts could we give, therefore, if we were more like the great Giver of all gifts?

NOTE

1. C. S. Lewis, "The Efficacy of Prayer," in *The World's Last Night and Other Essays* (New York: Harcourt Brace Jovanovich, 1960), 10–11.

Other Forms
of Poverty

A poverty of conception and perception leads, in turn, to a grim poverty of expectations. Living below this particular poverty line thus affects how people see themselves, God, life, others, and the universe.

When we are taught by the Holy Spirit, however, then we can see "things as they really are, and . . . things as they really will be" (Jacob 4:13). This expands *conception, perception,* and *expectation.* Each of these enlargements accelerates real conversion.

Yes, the economically poor are always with us, but so is this other form of poverty (Matthew 26:11). We are to minister to both.

GOD'S CAPACITY, OUR DEPENDENCY

The vastness of space and the personalness of God's love tell us of a God who is marvelous beyond all our powers of conception and expression. In fact, rather than worry about *how* He does it all, we should rejoice over the *why* of His purposes, individually and globally.

George MacDonald observed that some people are simply not capable of worshiping a god any greater than they can personally imagine.[1] With the equivalent of a Do Not Disturb sign hung in place, there are so many mortal comfort levels reached by following such little gods.

Finite minds, especially those with short spiritual memories, may think it does not make sense that the brass plates could be wrested from someone like mighty Laban (1 Nephi 3:12–13) nor that landlubber Nephi could build a ship (1 Nephi 17:17–18). But given God's incomparable capacity, we are to be meek enough to consider things that make uncommon sense. Especially given our lower ways, surely we mortals should not dismiss God's higher ways, as if we can gavel out of existence all that which we cannot comprehend (Mosiah 3:5).

NOTE

1. Rolland Hein, *George MacDonald, Victorian Mythmaker* (Nashville: StarSong, 1993), 333–34.

MODERN JOSHUAS

The Joshuas of the twenty-first century will be righteous fathers and mothers the world over. These are the unsung but nevertheless real heroes and heroines of our time.

Those who work at their marriages are much more likely to create homes that are not simply churning, hectic hotels. Children reared in such nurturing homes are less likely to be heady, selfish, and lovers of themselves more than God (2 Timothy 3:2–4).

There are no attention-getting press releases or news conferences held by such parents declaring, "As for me and my house, we will serve the Lord" (Joshua 24:15). The parenting process nevertheless occurs quietly and steadily and will speak for itself.

EVIL

Some have genuine difficulty acknowledging that real evil exists in the world. Latter-day Saints know evil is allowed as a part of Heavenly Father's plan in which God "gave commandments unto men, . . . being placed in a state to act according to their wills and pleasures, whether to do evil or to do good" (Alma 12:31).

Evil always constitutes direct deductions from human happiness and direct additions to human misery. No wonder scriptural words about evil are harsh. Thus, trying to rationalize evil—nothing is finally wrong or a crime—is not merely naive but terribly tragic (Alma 30:17).

The Holy Ghost helps us to sense the presence

of evil and also helps us to turn away from it. Still, evil is not an awful abstraction outside ourselves which we are powerless to resist and which we can handily blame when we ourselves choose to act amiss. "We all recognize, in our better moments at least, that much harm comes from our own imperfections, sometimes terribly magnified, like traffic deaths from haste and aggression and reluctance to leave the party too soon: those are temptations. At the same time there are other disasters for which one feels no responsibility at all, like (as Tolkien was writing) bombs and gas-chambers. . . . It is a mistake just to blame everything on evil forces 'out there.'"[1]

We are free to choose, but choices bring certain consequences, affecting us and others and bringing happiness or misery. Outcomes do follow decisions, even if we did not directly choose the outcomes and their many consequences. There are gradations, too, such as the difference between a child mistakenly touching a hot stove after being warned and a person with evil aforethought pulling a trigger that causes mass destruction.

Accountability and consequences vary dramatically, which is one reason God's warnings and commandments matter so much. He knows history and what horrors evil can bring to us, His children, whom He loves. He would spare us all that.

NOTE

1. T. A. Shippey, *J. R. R. Tolkien, Author of the Century* (Boston: Houghton Mifflin, 2000), 142.

THE FIRST AND SECOND COMMANDMENTS

Though the second commandment is "like unto" the first commandment (Matthew 22:39), it is nevertheless still the second. Though we are to love our neighbors, we are certainly not instructed to worship them with all of our hearts, souls, and minds (Matthew 22:37).

We seldom ponder the first commandment and its implications. Either it is skipped over lightly as a given or it seems too daunting even to ponder. In any case, so often it goes unexamined. Given our usually selfish mindsets, no wonder we do not hurry to get mental realignments. Can we really and fully keep the second commandment until the first is acknowledged and significantly kept?

Selfishness is self-worship. In its various gradations, it is a violation of the first commandment:
"Thou shalt have no other gods before me" (Exodus
20:3). Such selfishness can smother our chances of
keeping the second commandment. The problem is
further exacerbated when we act to "please ourselves" or even seek to set ourselves up "for a light"
(Romans 15:1; 2 Nephi 26:29).

The sequence of the first two commandments
on which "hang all the law and the prophets"
(Matthew 22:40) is important in yet another way.
The first commandment determines the metes and
bounds of orthodoxy, which, kept, then brings felicity by putting all other commandments and order-
ing principles in their proper place.

We rightly esteem certain other things as good,
but our regard for these should still be subordinated
to our love of God. Otherwise, we can elevate lesser
things—even though good things—into virtual and
demanding gods.

Anciently at least, the idols of wood and stone—
while objects of sincere devotion—were public
and out in the open, palpably displaying their
inanimate, immobile frailty. Not so transparent,

however, are the false gods of our own time; these can achieve an operational primacy that is subtle but very real. For example, there are our intense and persistent panderings for the praise of men or the worship of riches and power.

Hence, unless we place fundamental things in proper priority, we can be honorable, and we can do good, but still end up being incapacitated to receive "all that [God] hath" (D&C 84:38).

Deep inside our reluctance to worship God may be a reluctance to face the gap between ourselves and our own possibilities. What we *are* compared to what we have the power to *become* is not a measurement gladly pondered or undertaken by us very often. This avoidance is very human, to be sure, but it can reflect a costly form of stubbornness and can cause us to look "beyond the mark" of the first commandment (Jacob 4:14). As is the case so often, course corrections are needed.

THE PLAN OF HAPPINESS

In the plan of happiness, the Great Shepherd, Jesus, will neither drive nor even herd us along the straight and narrow path. Doing such would be against God's agency-drenched plan. Instead, exemplifying and beckoning, Jesus says, "Come, follow me" (Luke 18:22), the very words and the manner of a true Shepherd.

If, hypothetically, at the end of the journey we were to receive undeserved rewards, these would soon prove unsatisfying and unenjoyable, anyway (D&C 130:2). Besides, divine integrity precludes God's giving us unmerited blessings. Amid lives whipsawed by human frailties, we really wouldn't want God to cut corners. We want God to be God!

Only then can we truly worship Him. Even those who have lived "without God in the world" will one day confess that "he is God" (Mosiah 27:31). There will be no questioning of His reality, His character, or of His capacity then.

Meanwhile, strange, is it not, how we are willing to settle for so much less? We are like an eager child at a candy store who will settle for just "one of these and one of those," when the Owner desires to give us the whole store (D&C 84:38).

JOY FOR A SEASON

We can become highly specialized in our professions, vocations, and avocations wherein we can do much good. We can even have "joy . . . for a season" and yet still lack "one thing": full submissiveness to God (3 Nephi 27:11; Mark 10:21). Furthermore, receiving even the deserved plaudits of mankind can bring addicting adulation—an endangering substitute for what God desires to give us. For instance, an individual of integrity might not bear false witness, and yet never fully yield his mind to God! Another might bestow generous help on the poor but live as an adulterer.

In the ultimate and seamless symmetry of the

soul, there is no place for this patchwork of jarring jaggedness. True joy is everlasting, not just "for a season."

SELFISHNESS

Though often nearly saturated in selfishness and self-pity, yet we are told to become "even as Jesus is" (3 Nephi 27:27). How else can we first get out of this thick ooze, except we fully worship Him in whom there is no selfishness?

David, the mighty warrior, probably felt he "deserved" Bathsheba. But did Uriah therefore "deserve" to be betrayed both in his marriage and then on the battlefield? (2 Samuel 11:14–17). When Joseph in Egypt was tempted, he said he would not sin against God *nor* against Potiphar (Genesis 39:9–17). He understood his relationship with God as well as with his fellowmen, blending the two great commandments.

Selfishness causes us to be so acquisitive and possessive. We also like our own marquee, be it a noticed role or a signature specialty of some kind. We can easily be taken in by the almost caressing touch of the "praise of men" (John 12:43), emanating as it does from those who occupy the mortal galleries to which we earnestly play. Nevertheless, these are merely rented galleries, and the ushers of succeeding events will evacuate them again and again.

Selfishness and self-pity preoccupy us in ways that make the sincere pursuit of the two great commandments very difficult. Whereas some worked the crowd to cry for Barabbas instead of Christ, the adversary is also content to work a crowd of one.

GOD'S MERCY

The mercy of God is so personalized. Aaron's behavior in the golden calf episode was not his finest hour, yet later a priesthood was named after him (Exodus 32:1–6, 21, 24, 26). There are so many ways in which God demonstrates His long-suffering, mercy, and generosity, often by providing us with the necessary experiences of record, opportunities to learn fundamental spiritual truths for ourselves.

On the road to Emmaus, the resurrected Jesus could have told the two disciples at once with Whom they conversed. Instead, He let them learn later, upon reflection, what it meant to have had their hearts "burn" within them (Luke 24:32). How many times in the days to follow did those so tutored have cause to recognize and be guided by a burning in the bosom? (D&C 9:8).

THE GREAT QUESTION

In so many ways, we come back to the fundamental question, namely, do we believe in God, and, if so, what kind of God? In the New Testament, the operative inquiry was, "What think ye of Christ?" (Matthew 22:42). In the Book of Mormon, it is whether or not there really is a rescuing Christ. This constitutes the "great question" (Alma 34:5).

In responding to that great question, some stumble needlessly over the divine attributes of foreknowledge and omniscience. Finite man can scarcely understand the infinite capacity of God, yet we can be nurtured by the array of reassuring scriptures which so attest and which tell us—in micro and in macro ways—more than we can fully absorb:

"My name is Jehovah, and I know the end from the beginning" (Abraham 2:8).

"Before I formed thee in the belly I knew thee; and before thou camest forth out of the womb I sanctified thee, and I ordained thee a prophet unto the nations" (JST Jeremiah 1:5).

"Nevertheless God knoweth all things" (Mormon 8:17).

"But there is no God beside me, and all things are present with me, for I know them all" (Moses 1:6).

"I observed that they were also among the noble and great ones who were chosen in the beginning to be rulers in the Church of God" (D&C 138:55).

"The same which knoweth all things, for all things are present before mine eyes" (D&C 38:2).

"In the presence of God, . . . all things for their glory are manifest, past, present, and future, and are continually before the Lord" (D&C 130:7).

Revelation thus dramatically compensates for

our lack otherwise of full understanding about God's character!

Some believe in these and other relevant revelations; many do not. We are all left free to choose. Nevertheless, the "great question" remains; ignored or unanswered, it still refuses to go away, even if we turn away from it and from Him (Mosiah 3:5).

INTELLECTUAL HUMILITY

The meek but declarative wisdom of King Benjamin underlines the need for intellectual humility: "Believe that man doth not comprehend all the things which the Lord can comprehend" (Mosiah 4:9).

How can mankind comprehend the cosmos of God? "Worlds without number have I created. . . . But only an account of this earth . . . give I unto you"; "innumerable are they unto man; but all things are numbered unto me, for they are mine and I know them" (Moses 1:33, 35). "Behold, I am God. . . . Wherefore I can stretch forth mine hands and hold all the creations which I have made; and mine eye can pierce them also" (Moses 7:36).

The Prophet Joseph Smith said, "It is the constitutional disposition of mankind to . . . set bounds to the works and ways of the Almighty."[1]

How can finite man fully comprehend the "infinite atonement" anyway? (2 Nephi 9:7; Alma 34:12). Yet we mortals can still be deeply grateful for all that has been revealed about the Atonement. As its primary beneficiaries, we ought to be.

NOTE

1. Joseph Smith, *Teachings of the Prophet Joseph Smith,* sel. Joseph Fielding Smith (Salt Lake City: Deseret Book, 1976), 320.

CHEAP FAITH

Those who make only casual and vague efforts to develop faith will inevitably be disappointed. For example, without the study of the word, the nourishment flowing from the truths upon which faith is based is simply unreceived! Faith does not develop automatically.

The true believer, in contrast, develops specific faith in the Father's *plan* of happiness, faith in the straight and narrow *path* as shown by the character of the atoning Savior, and faith in the sobering *promises* made by God to His children. In this manner, true believers finally "overcome by faith" (D&C 76:53). They stand meekly before memories of

God's *past* blessings, because they have "proved him in days that are past."[1]

In contrast, the periodic musers who settle for a cheap faith are not actually prepared to do what the prodigal did: He "came to himself" and with conviction said, "I will arise and go to my father" (Luke 15:17–18). Persistent thought was followed by sustained action. He showed the determination to break with his pig-filled present in order to fashion a better and brighter future. Faith, indeed, is the moving cause of spiritual action.

Deficient mental effort and refusal to trust the Spirit, however, are the first causes of failure. Oliver Cowdery, for example, took no thought save it was to ask for the faith to translate; he did not continue as he commenced (D&C 9:5). Peter walked on a raging sea but did not continue, either.

Discipleship is a journey, not merely a starting line, as we soon learn. One day we shall learn that the real starting line was way back in the premortal recesses of our existence.

NOTE

1. *Hymns of The Church of Jesus Christ of Latter-day Saints* (Salt Lake City: The Church of Jesus Christ of Latter-day Saints, 1985), no. 19.

OVERCOMING BY FAITH

Among other things, a real disciple is willing, if necessary, to be part of a righteous behavioral minority, enduring the tauntings and cultural disapproval of those who walk in the wide and broad way. Such is part of the lot of the "few there be that find it" (Matthew 7:14; 3 Nephi 14:14).

By holding fast to the iron rod, disciples will not wander, nor will they give undue heed to the "fiery darts" (1 Nephi 15:24; 8:33). Clinging to the word of God on the sometimes mist-shrouded path is vital, but more is involved than clinging to the rod. Also required is pressing forward, even if one cannot always see the destination clearly and constantly

91

(1 Nephi 8:24). Disciples thus "overcome by faith" (D&C 76:53), not by traveling effortlessly on easy escalators.

Overcoming by faith consists of "keeping the commandments," that they might be "washed and cleansed from all their sins" and of being "sealed by the Holy Spirit of promise" (D&C 76:52–53).

Incessant mocking can, of course, cause less-settled believers to complain. It was so in the days of Malachi when some said, "It is vain to serve God" (Malachi 3:14), because disbelievers and mis-behavers seem to be "set up": "they dare God—and they escape" (Moffatt version, Malachi 3:15).[1] Unlike manna, divine justice is not meted out daily or visibly. Disciples understand this gospel ground rule.

NOTE

1. James Moffatt, *A New Translation of the Bible, Containing the Old and New Testaments* (New York: Harper and Brothers, 1935).

THE BLESSINGS
OF MEEKNESS

If we peeled away from our many verbal communications the ego-driven portion (things said thoughtlessly, or for effect, or to achieve advantage), how much substance would then remain?

Meekness serves us well in this respect and in so many others. When, for instance, we are overlooked or bypassed, we can easily feel slighted. Meekness emancipates us from such a reaction, because it neither regards others as rivals nor as objects of envy. Nor does meekness spend valuable time decoding incoming communications in anxious search of praise, criticism, or hidden meanings. Meekness also avoids that added fatigue brought on by the breathless pursuit of preeminence.

Meekness thus provides a peaceful sanctuary from all such storms. There is a further bonus: more time is made available by not always having to keep score, whether in an unsettled marriage in need of improved communication or in a competitive professional relationship.

Whether at the office roundtable or in our neighborhoods, it isn't that the meek always and automatically have better information. Rather, they draw strength from a much more fundamental assurance: they know that God loves them (1 Nephi 11:17). They also know that the Lord is just and is "no respecter of persons" (Acts 10:34), so they seek to please Him rather than playing for approval from the various niche galleries.

The meek are simply more free, more peaceful, and more cheerful.

REPENTANCE AND INTELLECTUAL ENLARGEMENT

The Greek word for repentance means to change one's mind, such as regarding one's view of God, life, the universe, himself, and his fellowmen (LDS Bible Dictionary, 760). Included in the good news of the restored gospel is that by thus changing one's mind, an eternal perspective is given to life's meaning.

Consider how, for many years, some have sincerely argued that resemblances between religious beliefs in different cultures are an evidence of man's aspirations, not of God's existence. The "good news" of the Restoration, however, includes dispensationalism, reminding us that Adam and Eve had the gospel in the beginning (Moses 5:58–59).

Later, the fragments of the original faith, shards of truth, were scattered across this planet. Of this pattern, President Joseph F. Smith said:

"Undoubtedly the knowledge of this law and of other rites and ceremonies was carried by the posterity of Adam into all lands, and continued with them, more or less pure, to the flood, and through Noah, who was a 'preacher of righteousness,' to those who succeeded him, spreading out into all nations and countries, Adam and Noah being the first of their dispensations to receive them from God. What wonder, then, that we should find relics of Christianity, so to speak, among the heathens and nations who know not Christ, and whose histories date back beyond the days of Moses, and even beyond the flood, independent of and apart from the records of the Bible."[1]

Another example of the good news of the Restoration is its enlarged and reassuring view of the universe in which Jesus is the creating Lord of the Universe (D&C 76:23–24). Vast as the cosmos is, however, Heavenly Father has told us that His work is focused on us—to "bring to pass the immortality and eternal life of man" (Moses 1:39).

Similarly, because individual and human history reflects the good and bad choices of mankind, the good news of the restored gospel is how the role of agency is undeviatingly central to Heavenly Father's plan. The bad choices are permitted but not endorsed by God. So the consequences of misused agency are to be expected. Of this, President Joseph F. Smith said:

"Many things occur in the world in which it seems very difficult for most of us to find a solid reason for the acknowledgment of the hand of the Lord. I have come to the belief that the only reason I have been able to discover by which we should acknowledge the hand of God in some occurrences is the fact that the thing which has occurred has been permitted of the Lord."[2]

NOTES

1. Joseph F. Smith, *Journal of Discourses,* 26 vols. (London: Latter-day Saints' Book Depot, 1854–86), 15:325.
2. Joseph F. Smith, "A Message to the Soldier Boys of 'Mormondom,'" *Improvement Era,* July 1917, 821.

DOCTRINAL
WHITE DWARFS

S o much meaning is compressed into the doctrines of the gospel. We dare not be superficial
or discouraged, therefore, by the unfolding-
ness in our understanding. The doctrines are like
the "white dwarfs" in the universe, which have so
much compressed matter that their density defies
our present understanding.

Certain doctrines of the kingdom are so full of
meaning and of personal significance that one can
only sense their full importance by accepting in
faith pronouncements of the Lord. Even though
some of their dimensions are now well beyond us,
neglecting these doctrines entirely is not the answer.

Illustrating deep implications are "Man was also

in the beginning with God" (D&C 93:29) and "All things for their glory are manifest, past, present, and future, and are continually before the Lord" (D&C 130:7). In the justice and mercy of God, we finally receive "according to [our] desires" (Alma 29:4).

We cannot process all the implications, because they bear upon us profoundly and personally. No wonder it is to be "line upon line" and "precept upon precept" (D&C 128:21)—and course correction upon course correction—so far as our personal comprehension and application are concerned. What an inexhaustible gospel!

BEING RULED OVER

Some are stubborn and revolt against *all* authority. Status-conscious, we may worry about whether a Moses or a Nephi is ruling over us (Numbers 16:2; 2 Nephi 5:3). This resistance to mortal authority—"ye take too much upon you"—by some is often extended to God, even though He generously lends us all breath from moment to moment (Numbers 16:3; Mosiah 2:21). Yes, respiratory capacity is provided by God even for rebels, who then use it without gratitude. Ironically, these individuals celebrate their independency without realizing how very dependent they actually are and from moment to moment.

STAGGERING NOT

Because the world is readily inclined to mock at divine promises, the promises inherent in the gospel can jar the ordinary intellect, bereft of faith.

Like Abraham, however, we know it is vital for us not to stagger at the soaring promises that God has made to us. The promises are so bold! But unwillingness to believe in those promises, ironically, keeps some from pursuing their great spiritual journey with real intent.

Paul wrote of the faith of Abraham and Sarah and the promises about their posterity when such advanced years made them "as good as dead." "But," he continued, "having seen [the promises] afar off, [they] were persuaded of them, and embraced them" (Hebrews 11:12–13).

The promise given Abraham about his impending posterity went against the obvious, but he did not stagger. If we ask ourselves what we are missing by being unable to see "afar off," it includes soaring things that can stagger the imagination if we do not possess adequate faith.

When we are too zoomed in on our own little vineyards, we may, as Jesus chided, successfully forecast the weather but still not discern the signs of the times (Matthew 16:2–4). Or, as the Lord said in 1831, prior to Civil War days, Americans felt there would be "wars in far countries" but did not know "the hearts of men in [their] own land" (D&C 38:29). We can perish, too, if tunnel vision is all we have.

No More Than a Particle

We cannot dilute the doctrines simply to make them easier to believe. We must face them head on and not be intimidated by their stunning implications. Yet when faith begins, it can be so small and precious a thing (Alma 32).

To sustain us in this great developmental adventure, we are helped by the fact that every gospel principle carries within itself its own witness that it is true. Nevertheless, faith may begin with no more than a particle of a desire to believe (Alma 32:27).

There is certainly no need to be embarrassed because of particle-like beginnings. Tiny seeds become seedlings, which in turn become trees. If we are doing our nurturing part, we will scarcely notice all the necessary growing seasons.

ENDURING AND STRETCHING

By its very nature, the process of enduring does not permit exemptions or shortcuts. Likewise, there can be no skipping of the relevant experiences. There can be no convenient deletion of the phrase "to the end."

Stretching our spiritual capacity takes time, but such enlargement is the essence of discipleship, and it is tied to our eternal happiness. We wouldn't really want to cut classes now anyway, if we knew how our future capacity would then be diminished. In sum, there is no auditing, because the classes are for credit.

Any recesses are very brief, and school is not out until the bell rings.

THE DISTRACTIONS AND DIVERSIONS OF THE WORLD

The garish and neon distractions of the world are very pervasive and invasive. Sometimes, it is as if we were strolling down a carnival row with the various diverting lures being constantly touted by circus barkers. A very different challenge is meeting the subtle allures of being culturally correct, as symbolized by the "great and spacious building" with all its finery, ambience, and seeming leisure (1 Nephi 11:36).

Amid both the above cacophony and subtlety is the "simpleness" and "easiness" of the way" (1 Nephi 17:41). It is strange how sign-seekers who anxiously search seem unable to read the most simple road markers.

"It Mattereth Not"

Disciples who care deeply about essential things also know how to handle the marginal things. The challenge may be managing undeserved criticism: "And now, in your epistle you have censured me, but *it mattereth not;* I am not angry, but do rejoice in the greatness of your heart" (Alma 61:9; emphasis added).

Or having less concern for whatever remains to do after we have done our major duties: "Therefore I will write and hide up the records in the earth; and whither I go *it mattereth not*" (Mormon 8:4; emphasis added). "Whether the Lord will that I be translated, or that I suffer the will of the Lord in the flesh, *it mattereth not,* if it so be that I am saved in the kingdom of God. Amen" (Ether 15:34; emphasis added).

Or coping with unreciprocated love: "And it came to pass that the Lord said unto me: If they have not charity *it mattereth not* unto thee, thou hast been faithful" (Ether 12:37; emphasis added).

Meekness and trust in God make possible the sincere utterance of the three words "it mattereth not." It is a spiritual posture that is knee bending, not shoulder shrugging.

VARIATIONS OF DENIAL

We can deny the Lord in so many ways: "They profess that they know God; but in works they deny him" (Titus 1:16).

"Yea, there were many churches which professed to know the Christ, and yet they did deny the more parts of his gospel" (4 Nephi 1:27).

"There shall be false teachers among you, who privily shall bring in damnable heresies, even denying the Lord that bought them" (2 Peter 2:1).

"But behold, I fear lest the Spirit hath ceased striving with them; and in this part of the land they are also seeking to put down all power and authority which cometh from God; and they are denying the Holy Ghost" (Moroni 8:28).

"Deny not the spirit of revelation, nor the spirit of prophecy, for wo unto him that denieth these things" (D&C 11:25).

When Samuel's counsel was rejected, he was reminded by Jehovah, "They [Israel] have not rejected thee, but they have rejected me" (1 Samuel 8:7).

The denials of lapsed disciples are especially sad: "Having denied the Holy Spirit after having received it, and having denied the Only Begotten Son of the Father, having crucified him unto themselves and put him to an open shame" (D&C 76:35). Significantly, these denials involve the three members of the Godhead.

Things have not really changed much, therefore, with regard to rejection of the Divine. Whatever the form of denial, we are diminished thereby.

SELFISHNESS AND PERMISSIVENESS

Whenever selfishness flexes, it victimizes. It bullies empathy and generosity, just as when pride pulsates, pushing away graciousness and meekness. The more we move away from submission to God, the more submissive we become, instead, to the selfish, natural man.

In contrast, because self has been tamed and gentled, keeping the two great commandments brings a flowering of empathy, mercy, loving-kindness, patience, meekness, generosity, purity, graciousness, and truthfulness.

Unlike submissiveness, permissiveness—at the end of its journey—stands empty, limp, and mute, trailing its awful consequences. Permissiveness assumes agency comes without responsibility, as if gravity were suspended; it then hopes that the judgments of God will be superficial (2 Nephi 28:8).

A CHURCH OF MAN

Who would really want to belong to a church that could be made over whimsically in one's own image? Of necessity, any such church would feature Playdough principles, pliable to the reshaping touch of eager and successive fingers. Its leaders would constantly risk incumbent fatigue.

The doctrines and commandments of men may have sway among some for a season, but they cannot survive the exposing light that "groweth brighter and brighter until the perfect day" (D&C 50:24).

Some relativists, who profane instead of profess Christ, might consider this searching query, "Are ye ashamed to take upon you the name of Christ . . . because of the praise of the world?" (Mormon 8:38). Another query is, "Whom say *ye* that I am?" (Luke 9:20; emphasis added), not "What did a focus group think of Christ?"

The answer to the real question cannot, finally, be delegated. As Peter experienced, reporting the attitudes of others was soon followed by the personalized "What think ye of Christ?" (Matthew 22:42).

Smiles and Shades

Even our simplest smiles are like parted shutters, emitting the soul-light of which there is no surplus in the world. Nevertheless, too many live as if boarded up, preferring to look out upon others rather than illuminating the scene themselves. Such tinted glass in its variations is a strange twist on seeing "through a glass, darkly" (1 Corinthians 13:12).

This distancing is scarcely consistent with the open, sunlit second great commandment. Privacy is rightfully cherished, of course, for providing needed renewal and respite, but not to cover sins. Yet there are selfish forms of privacy meant to insulate one from one's neighbors, constituting an assertion of individuality at the expense of keeping the second commandment.

Exemplars

Example has a special eloquence. Even when meekly expressed, it is nevertheless powerful. How blessed each of us is to know some exemplars, which includes those sincerely striving to be such (D&C 46:9). Imperfections being worked on "in process of time" are not disqualifications, therefore, any more than crusts of bread should be withheld simply because we cannot presently offer those in need a three-course meal.

Erring ones may quietly rein themselves in simply because of the presence of an exemplar. The latter can thus serve as a helpful restraint and can convey loving disapproval to the erring one. It is more than tongues can transmit.

A verbal observation can cause deep and needed introspection, as when those condemning the woman taken in adultery put down their stones, "being convicted by their own conscience" (John 8:9).

When we seek to stand against the surf of sin, however, let us do so without being puffed up, lest, being bloated, we ourselves are more easily carried away by the current.

AGENCY AND JOY

In the next world, we will finally receive what we have persistently desired and chosen during mortality (Alma 29:4). Individually, we will have made so many incontestable, on-the-record choices. The final outcome, therefore, will be perfectly just, and all mortals will so acknowledge (Alma 29:4; Mosiah 27:31). In effect, we will receive the degree of joy we have demonstrably chosen and which we have developed the capacity to receive.

But how can Heavenly Father, Himself, have a fulness of joy? Especially when some of His children, by then immortalized, have freely and finally chosen something other than eternal life with Him and Jesus?

After He blessed the Nephite children, Jesus could movingly say, "Now behold, my joy is full" (3 Nephi 17:20). He so declared, though aware that many in the world were not keeping His commandments and some even esteemed Jesus as "naught" (Helaman 12:6; Mark 9:12; Acts 4:11).

Only in the framework of faith in God's mercy and justice can we ponder the interplay of agency and joy so central to God's plan.

Of necessity, God's gift of agency operates in the context of genuine alternatives among which we choose. This is a condition fully consistent with God's plan of happiness. Without the very important condition of agency amid alternatives, life would be an undifferentiated "compound in one" (2 Nephi 2:11). God's creations would then be without real purpose, and His plan would certainly not be worthy of being called the plan of happiness.

Sadly, many of us use the grand gift of agency to choose things in conflict with obeying the first commandment. Hence, Peter tells us that whatever overcomes us, we are in "bondage" thereto (2 Peter 2:19). Only divine truth obeyed makes us eternally free, just as Jesus said (John 8:32).

At the end of the "day of this life" (Alma 34:32), which includes our making choices in the spirit world while awaiting the resurrection, God will have done all that He can to persuade us to choose maximum happiness and joy (D&C 138). With the final and full chance to accept the gospel in the spirit world provided "to all the spirits of men," the Lord of the Vineyard can ask the unanswerable question, "What could I have done more?" (D&C 138:30; Jacob 5:47).

THE AVAILABLE ATONEMENT

More of the Atonement is still available for us to apply individually. If we are meek enough, we will be churned by conscience and the Spirit as to past and present shortcomings, including our sins of omission as well as of commission. Divine discontent will cause us to draw even further upon the Atonement, bringing us thereafter supernal peace of conscience and healing.

Following repentance, full and lasting conversion brings a loss of "disposition to do evil" and, instead, a desire "to do good continually" (Mosiah 5:2).

Moving from *admiration* to *adoration* and on to *emulation* of Jesus simply cannot be accomplished and sustained without the spiritual energy emanating from real conversion. In the same way, a "hunger and thirst [for] righteousness" (Matthew 5:6) represents the development of a robust spiritual appetite.

We surely need the Savior's help to apply the Atonement's ongoing power, just as we need the Holy Ghost to achieve full conversion. Remarkable Peter's life tells us so much about full conversion.

TAKING AWAY THE STUMBLING BLOCKS

The restored gospel takes away certain stumbling blocks some encounter in developing faith in God and His purposes (1 Nephi 14:1). In place of the "plain and precious" doctrines of the gospel grew the stumbling blocks (1 Nephi 13:28), leaving inadequate explanations concerning, for example, the character of God and His purposes as well as the "why" questions about human agency and suffering. The absence of plain and precious truths brings intellectual impasses and impediments to developing faith.

Consider illustrative questions from those without an understanding of the plan of salvation: "If there is a God, and He is all powerful, why doesn't

He stop human suffering?" Or, "If there is a God, and He is righteous, why does He permit evil?" These questions cannot be responded to adequately without the fulness of the gospel (1 Corinthians 1:23; 10:13;1 Nephi 13:34; 2 Nephi 2:11; 26:20; Alma 12:28–30).

God is deeply committed to our free will, or moral agency. Yet the misuse of that agency causes much human suffering, about which many then complain. Without understanding the role of agency in the plan, we will not be able to understand human suffering. The lack of that understanding can, for some, be a real stumbling block (1 Nephi 14:1; Mosiah 23:21).

A refusal to heed the restored plain and precious things means the vexing stumbling blocks remain firmly in place. These include the very impediments over which philosophers have sincerely contended in so much of human history. Their removal is a matter of tremendous significance.

MORTAL STARS, IMMORTAL SOULS

Because of the Atonement, we are immortal! (1 Corinthians 15:22). The long-lived stars we see are not.

Though they have a longevity beyond our comprehension, the stars do finally expire, for "as one earth shall pass away, and the heavens thereof even so shall another come" (Moses 1:38).

God's "work and glory" are actually focused on our own immortalization, while providing the universe with planets to be inhabited, necessary to support His grand purposes for His children (Moses 1:39; Isaiah 45:18).

The psalmist praises the Lord, who "telleth the number of the stars; he calleth them all by their names" (Psalm 147:4; Isaiah 40:26). Thus, because of the reality of His omniscience and power, God's governance of the galaxies is possible.

The same psalmist speaks of yet another power of the Lord: how He "healeth the broken in heart, and bindeth up their wounds" (Psalm 147:3). God not only numbers the stars and knows their names but, more importantly, He knows us and our names, and He can heal our hearts and treat our wounds.

Though wide-eyed with wonder, we, being His spirit children, are not aliens in His universe.

CONVERSION

Jesus counseled Peter, "When thou art converted, strengthen thy brethren" (Luke 22:32). Yet impressive Peter had already had numerous spiritual experiences. He also had a testimony of Jesus and had so declared (John 21:15–16). Still, there remained the challenge of full conversion.

The virtues enumerated by Peter in his epistle and still earlier by King Benjamin are the same. Each is to be developed as part of achieving and reflecting conversion (2 Peter 1:5–7; Mosiah 3:19). For example, each of us has received "great and precious promises" (2 Peter 1:4). Nevertheless, those promises, if we are not faithful, can prove to be intimidating unless we are meek and humble.

Though full conversion is preceded by baptism, receiving the Holy Ghost, and having a testimony, it is a process which, over time, involves full submission to our Lord Jesus Christ and greater emulation of Him. We cannot expect real conversion or discipleship to be a one-time, one-ordinance, and one-act thing:

"And now, my beloved brethren, after ye have gotten into this strait and narrow path, I would ask if all is done? Behold, I say unto you, Nay. . . . Wherefore, ye must press forward with a steadfastness in Christ, having a perfect brightness of hope, and a love of God and of all men. Wherefore, if ye shall press forward, feasting upon the word of Christ, and endure to the end, behold, thus saith the Father: Ye shall have eternal life" (2 Nephi 31:19–20).

Seamless Love

We have been given needed and generalized teachings with regard to developing our capacity to love. Additional teachings are more particularized and alert us to certain of our flaws. Thus, our canopies of love can be much more seamless and less torn in places as we seek to spread them.

For instance, true love is "never glad when others go wrong" (Moffat version, 1 Corinthians 13).[1] What a subtle but stern test. Likewise, engaging in good works should not be "to please ourselves" (Romans 15:1). True love "envieth not" (1 Corinthians 13:4), including not envying those who seem to have no problems, when actually they are bearing heavy and unseen crosses.

Using candor without caring, we fail to speak the truth in love (Ephesians 4:15). Our candor then can leave others filled with "overmuch sorrow" (2 Corinthians 2:7). Love, however, takes into account the bearing capacity of others as well as our own capacity to show forth an increase in love to those we may reprove (D&C 121:43). President Brigham Young said we ought not "chasten beyond" our capacity to heal.[2]

Love is the key to the development of every other virtue, whether it is long-suffering, loving-kindness, or our capacity for meekness. Thus enlarged spiritually, we will not be "puffed up" because our souls are enlarged "without hypocrisy" (Moroni 7:45; D&C 121:42).

The flaws in our developing capacity to love can be repaired, if we are serious disciples. Our patchwork performance, though necessary, at first must later give way to a seamless saintliness.

NOTES

1. James Moffatt, *A New Translation of the Bible, Containing the Old and New Testaments* (New York: Harper and Brothers, 1935).
2. Brigham Young, *Journal of Discourses,* 26 vols. (London: Latter-day Saints' Book Depot, 1854–86), 9:124–25.

CONSCIENCE AND EMPATHY

For the meek, pangs of conscience are often felt quickly, for instance, when we have said something that should not have been said at all or said with much more sensitivity. If quickly informed of the miscue, we can proceed quickly and with rectifying regret.

The spiritual reproof is designed to get our attention while the episode is fresh. Why should we be surprised that it is so? No wonder working out our salvation is such serious and steady business. To be sure, realization often occurs later in subsequent pondering of things; we come to realize we could have done better. But the "here and now" calls of conscience are best heeded promptly.

We are free, of course, to brush aside such messages, but the more often these are deflected, the more emotionally encrusted we can become, even "past feeling" (Ephesians 4:19; 1 Nephi 17:45). Much as we regret having to feel stinging regrets, there is no other way.

Unsurprisingly, too, we sometimes find ourselves praying earnestly and in advance over how we might say or do something in order to be most helpful to others, something worth praying over. When we are successful in such anxious efforts, it is likely the helpful presence of our love that others feel more than any adroitness of our words. Others can easily forgive our verbal clumsiness when our love is present, but if love is not present, skillful words avail very little.

Even skillful diplomacy cannot substitute for genuine love.

GOD'S CHARACTER AND PURPOSES

Some things cause soul-flares. The faithful disciples in the storm-tossed small boat cried out, "Carest thou not that we perish?" (Mark 4:38). This and similar expressions demonstrate a failure to understand God's omniscient and perfect caring. Such questioning or wondering about the character of God reminds us of what the Prophet Joseph wisely said: "If men do not comprehend the character of God, they do not comprehend themselves."[1]

We can also fail to comprehend His purposes. In short, to some degree, like Laman and Lemuel, we may not understand the dealings of God with His children (1 Nephi 2:12; Mosiah 10:14). Hence, especially amid adversity, there is a tendency to "[charge] God foolishly" (Job 1:22). So much depends upon our understanding of Him and His purposes for us, lest we foolishly become angry with God. It is no overstatement, therefore, to describe such doctrines as "plain and precious things" (1 Nephi 13:28). Isn't it odd how their very plainness is off-putting to some who seek "for things that they [cannot] understand"? (Jacob 4:14). Could it be that such individuals prefer ambiguity to accountability?

NOTE

1. Joseph Smith, *Teachings of the Prophet Joseph Smith*, sel. Joseph Fielding Smith (Salt Lake City: Deseret Book, 1976), 343.

A Listening Heart

How vital is a "listening heart"! The heart hears feelings while the mind attends to words. Often, what we are feeling needs to be heard even more than what we say. Words may not give full disclosure, anyway. Having a listening heart is, therefore, such an advantage.

Consider the exchange between Jesus and the man who wanted an increase of faith so that his son might be healed of his disability. Jesus responded to the man's petition for help, "If thou canst believe, all things are possible to him that believeth."

The man replied, "Lord, I believe." Then, almost immediately, came the anxious confession of the man's further concern: "Help thou mine unbelief" (Mark 9:23–24).

It was a moment of precious candor. Jesus had the perfect listening heart to heal the boy and help the father.

THE MIND OF MAN

The mind is a natural battlefield. Because the word of God is "more powerful" than anything else, it only adds to the fierceness of the fray (Alma 31:5). The requirement inherent in agency remains: "Let every man be fully persuaded in his own mind" (Romans 14:5).

Some warning signs are posted. People think they are wise when they are learned, so they decide not to heed the counsel of God (2 Nephi 9:28–29).

Likewise, a mind can spurn the "plain and precious things" in favor of sophistry, or by favoring complexity (1 Nephi 13:28; Jacob 4:14). King Benjamin was quick to see this and warned that we must realize we cannot comprehend all the things

God comprehends (Mosiah 4:9). The mind can otherwise have difficulty getting "outside the box" unless revelation is accepted, as when Moses learned things he "never had supposed" (Moses 1:10).

The mind can become "hardened in pride" (Daniel 5:20; Habakuk 1:11). And it can also engage in self-deception, as Korihor finally acknowledged (Alma 30:48–50). The mind can let itself become defensively compartmentalized, a fortress astride the path to faith.

Insulating part of the mind violates Jesus' injunction, "Thou shalt love the Lord thy God with all thy heart, and with all thy soul, and with *all thy mind*" (Matthew 22:37; emphasis added).

God is fully aware of our thought processes. "Thus saith the Lord . . . for I know the things that come into your mind, every one of them" (Ezekiel 11:5).

An active mind can be submissive without being passive: "Be ye transformed by the renewing of your mind, that ye may prove what is that good, and acceptable, and perfect, will of God" (Romans 12:2; Alma 32).

Hence the great importance of searching and receiving God's word: the scriptures, revelation, and living prophets. If we exclude these superb sources, then our database is dramatically shrunken and we will end up surveying the inside of so many small envelopes. The latter is hardly an adequate response to the Prophet Joseph's invitation:

"The things of God are of deep import; and time, and experience, and careful and ponderous and solemn thoughts can only find them out. Thy mind, O man! if thou wilt lead a soul unto salvation, must stretch as high as the utmost heavens, and search into and contemplate the darkest abyss, and the broad expanse of eternity—thou must commune with God. How much more dignified and noble are the thoughts of God. . . . None but fools will trifle with the souls of men."[1]

NOTE

1. Joseph Smith, *Teachings of the Prophet Joseph Smith,* sel. Joseph Fielding Smith (Salt Lake City: Deseret Book, 1976), 137.

REPENTANCE AND HOLY WORKS

God says that He reveals His plan episodically where mortals have faith (Alma 12:28–30). Why not reveal it more widely and often? Is it because God does not want to increase human accountability without a corresponding chance to change human behavior? Or is it that some, like Laman and Lemuel, simply do not understand? Or that still others have actually willed their deprivation by not really wanting to understand? Or is it because secular conditioning is so effective that the holy things of the Spirit are actually viewed as foolishness to be trampled upon? (Matthew 7:6). Only in the spirit world, it appears, will "all the spirits of men" receive either a first, full, or last chance to hear the gospel (D&C 138:30).

Alma, in describing how important God's plan of salvation is, addressed the consequences if man were to receive immortality "having no preparatory state" (Alma 12:26). In this preparatory state, among other things, we should be taught the difference between the holy and the profane and learn for ourselves the difference between the bad and the good (Ezekiel 44:23). We learn other things by our own experience. Thus, we can be indelibly described by what we have learned in the preparatory state rather than merely experiencing the fleeting intellectual attachments to this or that idea as we move along the mortal trail.

So vital is man's knowing about the plan of salvation that God has—under certain conditions and from time to time—sent angels, conversed Himself with man, and has otherwise made the plan of salvation known (Alma 12:30). Yet He has done it according to the faith, repentance, and holy works of the recipients.

Why the restraint? Do we really think the people of Sodom and Gomorrah in their last stages would have paid much attention to holy words or to a discussion of the plan of salvation?

Instead, the Lord has chosen to place the gospel seed in "good ground," being those with an honest and good heart who hear the word (Luke 8:15). An individual is good ground because he or she "heareth, understandeth, and keepeth" the word—to which the Prophet Joseph Smith added "and endureth" (Matthew 13:20, 23; JST Matthew 13:21; Matthew 5:6).

So much depends, therefore, upon this spiritual good ground rather than on thoughtlessly broadcasting the gospel seed without reference to the receiving soil.

RECEIVING APPLAUSE
AND TAKING BOWS

So often in life, when we are blessed to be able to contribute, to achieve, and to help others, we take our bows and receive applause and acclaim. It takes a special meekness, however, to recognize that the bows we take and the applause we receive should go to God. Yet if we bow before Him and are meek about our achievements, then our vicarious role does not matter. Why should it, when He truly delights to honor those who serve Him? (D&C 76:5).

WHAT IS ALLOTTED TO US

While we are expected to improve our lot by developing our talents, using our gifts, and stretching our capacity to serve, it is clear that some of life's general circumstances constitute what is "allotted" to us (Alma 29:3). As to the latter, we are urged by the prophet Alma to be "content" with what is allotted to us (Alma 29:3, 6). It is no use, for example, desiring the voice of a trump to ensure a greater influence on mankind than one's circumstances permit. Hence the consoling and concluding words: "Why should I desire more than to perform the work to which I have been called?" (Alma 29:6).

Again, subject to our need to stretch and to

better ourselves, especially spiritually, there is no justification for perpetual resentment or restlessness, which keep us from being "content" with what is "allotted" and often unused. Such contentment is a form of meekness, because we are willing to wait upon the Lord's allotments and His timetable. We are strongly encouraged by various scriptures to touch those within our present circle of influence rather than obsessively wishing for a larger circle.

HOPE

"Faith is the *substance* of things hoped for, the *evidence* of things not seen" (Hebrews 11:1; emphasis added). Therefore, wrote Alma, "If ye have faith ye hope for things which are not seen, *which are true*" (Alma 32:21; emphasis added). Gospel hope is thus not naivete but rests on revealed assurances.

What is to be the focus of our fundamental hopes? Not the outcome of an athletic contest, a date, the condition of the stock market, nor even the ebb and flow of international politics. Instead, "I say unto you that ye shall have hope through the atonement of Christ and the power of his resurrection, to be raised unto life eternal, and this because of your faith in him according to the promise" (Moroni 7:41).

Such should be the focus of our ultimate hope, even though proximate hopes are understandably and often worthily present in our hearts and minds. Because of the Atonement and Resurrection, we can actually have a "brightness of hope" and "with surety hope for a better world" (2 Nephi 31:20; Ether 12:4).

Despair is found among those who are "without Christ, having no hope, and without God in the world" (Ephesians 2:12). Hence, as Peter counseled, disciples should "*be ready always to give an answer* to every man that asketh you a reason of the *hope* that is in you" (1 Peter 3:15; emphasis added).

Hope has its own way of being noticed, especially when accompanied by good cheer.

ORTHODOXY

Orthodoxy keeps the powerful doctrines of the revealed gospel in careful and much needed balance. Otherwise, if focused upon singly and exclusively, these doctrines are so powerful we can spin off and go wild. Orthodoxy, therefore, rather than being repressive, is a great adventure in handling powerful doctrines that bring great happiness when "fitly framed" and woven together but which can bring misery if we spin them off separately (Ephesians 2:21; 4:16). When doctrines are pulled apart from each other by mankind's selections, interpretations, and implementations, the results can be tragic.

Ultimate orthodoxy—and *orthodoxy* isn't a

popular word nowadays—is expressed in the Christlike life that involves both mind and behavior. Christ's manner of life is truly "the way, the truth, and the life" (John 14:6), and He has directed us to pursue his example (Matthew 5:48; 3 Nephi 12:48; 27:27).

The doctrines of the Church need each other as much as the people of the Church need each other. We dare not break the doctrines apart or specialize within them, because we need them all to achieve spiritual symmetry, an outcome that requires connections and corrections.

Orthodoxy is felicity—in beliefs and behavior.

INDEX